How t(

your home daily in
just minutes:

The complete guide to
creating a decluttered
home and life easily
and effortlessly.

Mary Hodges

THANK YOU NOTE

CHAPTER 1. INTRODUCTION

Welcome aboard

Congratulations for making that tough decision! It is never easy to get rid of stuff you have had for years and have grown attached to. However, there comes a time when you realize that most of these items are total 'junk' and merely 'space thieves'. You look at that dress hanging on the closet rail for two years already, hoping that you will gain some weight and maybe one day fit into it. Or you stare at that gift you received for your birthday and simply can't give away, (because it's wrong to dispose of a gift). Sometimes, it is a faulty kitchen appliance that you spent a fortune on and can't imagine disposing of it, but would rather let it be a monument in the kitchen. But it remains a reality that all these items are in fact junk!

The good news is that you got your hands on this book with the intention and determination to convert your house to a clutter-free home. It indeed excites me to know that the decision to de-clutter your home comes from within. I am over the moon that you are embarking on a minimalist lifestyle that will result in you dumping some of your favorite and treasured items.

Kudos to you! In a few months, you will be grateful that you gave up your hoarding habit.

Why?

Because your messy and cluttered home could be the reason why you always felt overwhelmed, stressed, anxious and helpless. But that is soon going to change, as we are on a journey to detox your home and revitalize your life.

WARNING! The declutter journey is not always an easy and smooth ride; it requires commitment and self devotion! Let's take the plunge and enjoy the ride!

Are you ready? Right! Time to take off!

Brief

Now that you have committed to declutter your home, I can't be happier for you. There is no reason to feel bad about your cluttered home or hoarding habit. Hoarding is normal and some people are actually born hoarders - also labelled aspack-rats. In fact, some studies suggest that hoarding is genetic and many people acquire it from previous generations.

Anyway, I'm not suggesting that you are a hoarder, but the fact remains that you have clutter at home that needs throwing out. Let us go ahead by understanding the basics.

What is clutter?

Everyone talks about clutter. It can be a cluttered life, a cluttered home, a cluttered room, etc. A quick Google search brought me to this:

clut·ter
/ˈklətər/ ◄)

Noun
A collection of things lying about in an untidy mass.

Verb
Crowd (something) untidily; fill with clutter.

Synonyms
confusion - muddle - mess - disorder - muss - jumble

Thus, in layman language, clutter is anything disorganized and untidy in your home. From my understanding, a delayed decision to get rid of *anything disorganized and untidy* brings about a cluttered home. Don't you agree?

Types of clutter

There are many types of clutter, but let us focus on the four main culprits:

1. **Rubbish**: Yes, you've got it right - rubbish! Perfectly ready to be thrown into the bin! It includes expired food and spices, broken appliances or anything that is no longer in use. You either fix them or you save your precious space for storage of respectable items.

2. **Overflowing stuff**: If confronted with an overflow of items,, it simply means that you have limited space and do not have the means to store everything. Think of a child's drawer overflowing with toys. My friend, time has come to scale down and to get rid of every unused toy and toys your child has outgrown. To invest in an additional piece of furniture to store the toy, shouldn't be an option at all be. You will simply be swamping an already overcrowded space.

3. **Stuff that belongs to other people**: Do you have friends and relatives visiting you and leaving piles of stuff behind in your house? And what about the library books and other items you meant to return to a certain store, but have not yet found the time to do it. Now is the time to take that deliberate step to deliver these items to where they rightfully belong.

4. **Out-of-date tech**: You probably have an old cell phone, camera, computer or other tech devices that you clutch onto with dear life? If you no longer use them, now is the perfect time to cut your ties with them. Do a search and look around for the different options you have: - you can sell them online or locally, donate them or take them to a recycling collection point near you.

What Causes Clutter?

As already established, clutter is not only the disorganized and unnecessary stuff cramming the space on your floor - anything that gets between you and the life you'd rather be living, is CLUTTER. But what exactly initiates this clutter?

How does this clutter accumulate in our homes and we only figure it out when the clutter is already far too much?

According to declutter experts and professional organizers, the following three factors are the major contributors to a cluttered home.

1. Impulse buying

This is not a once off occurrence! How many times have I been guilty of buying something that I don't really need. It can be another brown cardigan or an extra two pairs of black flats: only to reach home to find a full closet with no space to accommodate the new entries.

After realizing that recreational shopping was the major culprit of clutter in my home, I however drastically changed my shopping habits.

You are most probably another victim of this debilitating habit! The best way to curb this, is to try and stay away from stores and shopping malls unless you desperately need to get something.

Besides, if it is essential for you to go, make a habit of only carrying enough cash on you to pay for your necessities. And please take heed to leave your credit cards at home; this way you can avoid this irresistible temptation!

2. Emotional attachment

We all possess those cherished items that we are not prepared to lose owing to their sentimental value.. A priceless shell collection of your Hawaii beach vacation ten years ago or several boxes filled with comic books, could be the culprits of causing clutter in your home.

To be honest, the memories they bring back, only occurs form time to time. There is no law that rules that you should toss away everything, but it is for you to determine which items you merely keep for sentimental reasons.

Obviously, you would want to keep clinging g to things you deem important to you. The calamity is when you are emotionally attached to each and everything in that home. The solution is to ask yourself one simple question: 'If I accidentally lost it, would I feel the pinch?'

3. Keeping what you no longer use

Do you keep things 'just in case' you might need them in future? You biggest concern is that you might discard them only to need them at some point in the future. It is a reality that each and everything in our homes can come in handy someday, but also the naked truth that 'someday' rarely comes!

If you start digging into your house, you will find piles of items that you hardly ever use. It could be that kitchen gadget you boxed after upgrading to the newer and more powerful one or your child's clothes that no longer fit. Make this the moment to let it go!

Engage in a weekly throw away session of 10 things you no longer use. If you have not used an item in the past year, the odds are that you will not need it in future.. Take action and dispose, sell or donate them. That is the best solution to avoid a home filled with 'just in case' things that is the main cause of clutter!

Possible reasons why you find it hard to declutter

1. The guilt feeling

Are you feeling guilty of losing that expensive coffee maker you bought fifteen years ago?

Or are you feeling wasteful getting rid of that ugly sweater you've never worn that rand ma knitted for you months ago?

Or is it the family heirloom that was passed to you by your late uncle?

I feel for you; we have all experienced this! And for sure, it's very hard to dispose of such valued possession.

But remind yourself of one thing; if you are keeping the item for the sake of its monetary value, the money has already been spent. And clinging onto it, will neither bring back your cash, nor add any value to your life.

If you are feeling wasteful binning that still new but ugly sweater, just remind yourself that you would have worn it if you were in love with it. The best way out will be to consider donating or selling it to someone else who will find it valuable.

Lastly, never feel obligated to keep something. This is your home and you should resist pressure to keep your home cluttered. We all have special friends and relatives who are nice enough to shower us with heartfelt gifts, but are we obliged to keep them?

If someone has given you a gift, appreciate the intention behind it and show gratitude towards the giver. What you decide to do with the gift afterwards, is solely your decision. And guilt should **never** play a part in your decision to keep or get rid of the gift! **Never**

If you feel that the 100-year old family Bible you inherited from your father is no longer of significant value, rather offer it to another family member who will treasure it. If they regard it as valuable, they will keep it. If not the case, just dispose of it, especially if you believe it's neither important nor useful any longer.

2. The opinion that lots of stuff can help you feel safe and secure

Sometimes our biggest concern about decluttering, is that we will not have enough when we need it. This is a typical scarcity mindset that keeps us hanging onto things that adds no value to our lives. Even when we don't really fancy some of the stuff, the notion that it gives us a sense of security, can make decluttering hard for a person.

Free yourself from this mindset and stop fretting!

You are not going to throw everything out, but you are just getting rid of the stuff that you no longer use and that you do not seriously favor. Too much stuff actually hinders the neat organizing of your home and consequently leaves you more stressed and strained. A decluttering exercise in fact creates more space in you home and gives you the freedom to enjoy that what adds value to your life.

3. No time to declutter

It makes perfect sense to me! Your mind and soul is willing to declutter, but your body does not want to cooperate. Life can become so busy that it turns into a struggle to find time to tidy up your home.

But with commitment, persuasion and dedication, it is still doable to declutter your home amidst a very tight schedule.

Even if it is only 5 or 10 minutes per day, be diligent and get rid of things that you no longer want in your home. Initially it might look like a slow process, but over time you will begin to see notable results.

Another trick would be to keep a keen eye on clutter as you go about your daily When you come across something you need to discard, immediately add it to the decluttering box. If you do this every day, you will soon be happy with your progress. The main thing is to just get started!

4. Not sure what to do with the stuff you are decluttering

Being unsure of where to take your decluttered items, makes most of us hesitant to declutter. If you can identify with this, later in this book I have an entire chapter detailing what to do with your items after decluttering. Generally however, you can plan to bin them for recycling, donate them or just turn them into cash.

NOTE! Once you acknowledge what is holding you back from letting go of clutter in your home, it will be easy to overcome the decluttering roadblocks.

15 Benefits of Decluttering your Home

You should by now be convinced that decluttering of your home will be the ultimate resolution for you. You might however still feel hesitant; it is normal and you shouldn't feel guilty about it. Remember, I warned you that this journey is going to be tough but not impossible?

In this section we shall hence take a look at fifteen reasons why decluttering your home will have a positive impact in your life.

1. You will enjoy more space
This is obviously the first benefit you will take great delight in. Unnecessary décor, chock-full closets and unused furniture can make you feel unsettled. And although you have worked hard to earn everything you possess, your main priority should be to feel comfortable in your home. The detoxing of your home will not only provide you with more living space, but will also make your guests feel more welcome.

2. You will be safer and healthier
A messy and disorganized home poses a potential danger to you and your family. Extreme clutter can easily become the ideal breeding ground for bugs and airborne viruses. In extreme cases it can turn into a fire hazard. A horde of unused stuff in the house, undoubtedly attracts dirt, chemicals and pet dander; a sure way to trigger allergies to all who live under your roof! With tons of stuff around, it is much harder to constantly keep your home clean and dust free. There will always be that unattended box of books or bin of toys that never gets the ne-

cessary attention.

3. Clutter causes stress

Studies have shown that the stress hormones of people often accelerates when they walk into a cluttered environment. The human mind always feels distracted in a cluttered area, simply because every part of the brain represents a task that needs to be completed. A cluttered home keeps inundating your brain with 'WORK! WORK! WORK!' That is much too exhausting and stressful.

Have you ever wondered why meditation is never performed in a disorganized and messy area? It makes sense that Buddhist monks meditate in beautifully manicured settings? Hopefully, you now understand the answer.

4. Clutter is a timewaster

Do you know that eliminating clutter can reduce your home cleaning with up to 40%? Clutter means that you are forever organizing and reorganizing your home. And yet a few minutes later, the house looks like it has never been cleaned.

Decluttering affords you time to focus on other important things other than just taking care of your home. You can actually now start a small farm, dive into your passion hobby and even get to spend more precious time with family and friends.

5. Declutter often awards you with the discovery of lost treasures

Decluttering means you'll be digging deep into every corner of your home in order to uncover any clutter that could be hiding somewhere. Often you will be fortunate enough to detect lost treasures that you had actually forgotten about. Your findings could also include some cash, never deposited checks and gift cards you probably stuck away and had totally forgotten about. Who wouldn't love some free money in times of a very tough economy?

6. Decluttering yields a sense of confidence and com-

petency

Decluttering puts into action your decision-making and problem- solving skills. Verify this: you have A, an amount of space and B, an amount of stuff. You need sound judgment to decide what to discard and what to spare. A successful judgment obviously boosts your confidence in your decision-making skills and self confidence.

7. You get to become better organized

Securing a place for all your possessions, is absolutely life-changing. An organized home makes it easier and quicker to locate whatever you are looking for. Cleaning and tidying an organized home is also much easier and quicker. Does this not make decluttering a wonderful consolation?

8. More storage space for you

Less stuff equals less hustling and stressing about enough storage space. Instead of worrying about your disorganized garage, you can now comfortably make room for an extra car in the compound.

9. Decluttering improves your social life

Nobody wants to invite people to a disorganized home. After decluttering, you become proud of your now clean and organized home and makes it pleasant to invite friends for a visit with a light heart. It also alleviates the worries about those unexpected visitors.

10. You become more disciplined

Decluttering teaches you valuable life lessons. The pain of forfeiting expensive gadgets that were in fact of no use to you, will in future make you a smarter and more disciplined buyer. You will now instead seriously consider the validity of every purchase, before spending money on it. Decluttering will assist you to attach more value to space than the hoarding of material possessions. Before embarking on any purchase, you will now first question the availability of space in your home. You could surely have enough money for a new dinner set, but however not have enough space for it. It is now that your self-discipline needs to kick in!

11. Decluttering improves your love life

If you are single, it's much sexier to bring a potential candidate to a clean environment than to a disorganized home space.

If you are married or in a relationship, your partner will much more appreciate living with a tidy person than one who is constantly collecting clutter.

In fact, decluttering can also be instrumental in the improvement of your sex life. A messy and disorganized home often leads to constant and unpleasant arguments concerning lost items, forgotten errands and disarray in general. All these conflicts can be avoided when you have a clutter-free home.

Always keep in mind that your living space is a reflection of who you truly are. Be careful of the message you are conveying to other people with regards to your lifestyle.

12. You create minimal trash

When you stay in an organized home, you consume less. By consuming less, you definitely create less trash. It is sad how our consumerist society is damaging the planet with too much garbage. Decluttering ensures that you only possess what you can comfortably manage in your small home.

13. Decluttering saves you money

There are three ways in which decluttering saves you money:

a. You will no longer purchase items on impulse. Burying a precious gadget to keep stowed away in a drawer at home, will become something of the past.

b. The fact that the space in your home is now clean and organized, will help you shy away from buying items that will turn into clutter.

c. You can sell some of the items you've decluttered. (Selling of clutter will be discussed in another section.)

14. You will reduce the burden on your children

As discussed earlier, some of our families have had family heirlooms for decades. We then presume that our future generations will be happy to inherit past family treasures. This is however not always the case! The younger generations of today, focus on living a minimalist life and heirlooms can become a burden to them. Never assume that your children are keen on inheriting any heirlooms, but rather discuss it with them and make plans accordingly. Either get rid of the stuff or pass it on to other family members.

15. You are able to help others by means of donations

There are hundreds of needy families in our society. When decluttering your home, you can donate some of your assets or unused items to charity. It is a win-win situation; you help out a needy person and enjoy a clutter-free home in return for your donation.

Valuing Space over Clutter

Allow me to digress just a little bit.

I love food - yes, I love good food; both healthy and unhealthy. I have a great weakness for pizza and given the chance, I would eat pizza every single day. Pizza is my comfort food; the preferred food one eats when one is tensed, bored or anxious.

Comfort food tastes heavenly, but once I've had enough, the good feeling disappears. My fondness for pizza however causes a lot of frustration and upheaval in my life. Currently, all my jeans are too small for me. The disappointment leaves me with frustration that leads to anxiety that cries out loud for more pizza. What a horrible cycle that I am trying to fight!

Let's get back to the clutter lessons!

Comfort food is very much comparable with comfort clutter. You might for example want to give the baby cot that your children slept in to your daughter in fifteen years from now.

Or you have a desire to use the old shoeshine box from the yard sale for the capturing of memorable photos where your children polish each other's shoes.

But as much as your idea is noble, there is not enough space for these valuable assets in your home. They consequently end up into your assorted pile of 'maybe' get riddance of. Much like my comfort food, this comfort clutter becomes a frustration when cleaning the house or when looking for things you actually need.

Although you regard all items entering your home as valuable, it is the opposite when they become part of a jumbled and disorganized mess. Everything but a pleasing sight to lay eyes on! Deciding on what to discard in that pile of Deciding what items to discard from the random pile of goods might not be easy, but is always achievable.

Start off by going through the pile of valuable stuff. You will be be shocked to discover that the ratio between the most valuable and non valuable possessions is 1:10. This implies that there are ten useless items for every potential valuable item.

Now is the time to value space above clutter; go ahead and discard all the non valuables!

Once you are done decluttering, you will delight in the open space you now have available. Imagine the feeling of bliss when you open drawers and shelves to find them organized and orderly with only a few items.

It will now be a pleasure to open the kitchen cabinets and easily grab your desired item without having to move other items out of the way and without the fear of things falling out of the cupboard.

Life becomes so much easier when you have a spacious home.

Valuing Space over Money

How many times have you grabbed amazing deals for things you don't need in the present but 'might' need in the future?

Sometimes we even engage in bargain shopping and end up taking things home that we would never use or need. (But you keep them anyway, as your friend's friend might be delighted to own them).

We tend to focus so much on ways to save, that we forget to be mindful of the limited storage space we have back home.

Many times you have enough money at your disposal to purchase new furniture for your home. It is however more important to question yourself and to check if you have enough space for an additional set of furniture.

Sometimes we keep ranting about our homes being too small, but the truth is that there would be ample space if we get rid of all the clutter.

Let's focus on the value of enough room and ample space to move around without bumping into stuff.

Sooner or later you will realize the monetary value of space. If you have a home that is spacious, you won't have the need to upgrade to a bigger house. In fact, you might even consider downsizing to a smaller home. Sufficient space translates to money that you would have spent on storage facilities for stuff that you most probably would have never used. If you value space as the main priority, your home will be your comfort zone and feel big and homely.

CHAPTER 2. DECLUTTERING ROOM BY ROOM

I n this chapter we will focus on ways to efficiently detox and declutter every room in your home. As we already know, this exercise won't be the most entertaining and fun-filled part. It'll be a cumbersome job. If you desire an organized home, you will have to jump in and do what you have to do!

You will find it surprising that even the holy book, the Bible, advocates decluttering. And if you don't believe it, here is the proof:

Ecclesiastes 3:6 "To every thing there is a season... a time to keep and a time to cast away."

To succeed, you don't need any fancy and expensive tools for the decluttering exercise. The most essential items for the exercise include the following:

1. Five to six baskets and bins (you can also get more; depending on the size of your decluttering exercise)
   a. The putting away of items that have crept out of their places
   b. The recycling of items such as paper, plastic and glass
   c. The fixing and mending of items that require further tinkering (for example, a pair of sandals that you love, but need mending or cleaning)
   d. The trashing of stuff that belongs in the bin

  e. The sorting of stuff that needs to be donated to friends, relatives or a charitable organization.
2. Rubber gloves
3. Cleaning rags
4. Step stool and small ladder to reach higher places
5. Basic household cleaning supplies
6. A notebook for notes of any items you might need to purchase (for example, organizers).

If you are still uncertain and undecided as to what to discard from every room, the questions below will help you to make a solid decision.

10 Questions to ask Yourself before Decluttering

1. *Do I love this thing?* If you don't, discard it
2. *Does it really make my life easier or harder?* If the latter is true, trash it
3. *Does it fulfill a purpose in my home?* If not, get rid of it
4. *Have I worn it for the past one year?* If not, let go of it
5. *Is it faulty or broken beyond repair?* If yes, toss it
6. *Am I keeping it out of guilt?* If yes, discard it
7. *In the case of books, magazines and videos - is the information outdated?* If so, let them go
8. *Do I already own something similar or almost similar?* If yes, declutter
9. *Am I spending too much time weighing its pros and cons?* If yes, into the trash bin
10. *Is it a reflection of the person I am today?* If it reflects a version of you from the past, let it go

Decluttering the Kitchen

Our kitchens are often the catchall room in the home. We spend most of our time in the kitchen cooking, eating or socializing. It is more like the family room in most homesteads. Therefore, a clean and clutter-free kitchen might truly appear like the magical dream.

But how many times have you walked into a friend's house and was amazed by how organized it was?

It is indeed very possible to achieve an organized appearance despite your jam-packed surfaces and cabinets. It's all a matter of being practical and realistic.

To begin this mission, I will guide you through the decluttering of the various spaces in your kitchen.

1. The Cabinets and Drawers

Cabinets are the primary storage area for most items in the kitchen: from rom foodstuffs, crockery, cookware, spices, kitchen tools, containers and many other nitty-gritty items. We will therefore take a broad look into this area - probably with more focus on the kitchen than any other area in your home.

Always use paper, vinyl or rubber cabinet liners to keep the shelves clean. And just in case you wonder why you need to declutter and reorganize the kitchen cabinets, here are more than enough valid reasons:

- You will no longer buy duplicates and this will be a money-saver. Yes, because you will always know what you have on hand.
- It will save time as you will always know where everything is stored.
- Meal planning and grocery shopping will become easier as you will always know what ingredients you have available.
- Cooking becomes easier when kitchen tools, missing bowls and measuring cups are conveniently placed.
- Your guests and family members feel more at home when they can easily locate everything in the cabinets.

Let us hence look at the main areas of focus on when decluttering the cabinets.

Extra crockery you never use: If your kitchen carries more cups, mugs, dishes and glasses than you probably need, it's time to donate the extras the needy. Some of us keep extra dishes just in case we need them someday we might have plenty of visitors. If you have not used them in the past two or three years, rest assured that the 'someday' will never arrive.

Plasticware: Plastic has become a part of our daily lives and the kitchen is no exception. No matter how unsafe plastic is, we still find ourselves using it for storage, cooking and even for packing of food on the go. Apart from being unsafe, plastic creates a lot of clutter because of its disposable nature. If possible, get rid of all your plastic items and embrace more environmentally friendly materials.

If it is a big deal for you to completely ditch your plastics, then at least manage them properly. If you for instance keep plastic cutlery and spatulas, discard them and replace them with metallic or wooden utensils.

It is a big an irritating annoyance that plastic lids often get lost and the cabinet becomes a nasty jumble of containers. Take the plunge and get rid of any container without a lid and consider purchasing a stackable set of containers to keep them organized.

Forget about the expensive bottled water and use filtered tap water in a BPA free bottle or reusable glass container.

When it comes to shopping bags, avoid the single use plastic bags that tend to accumulate in the kitchen and creating more clutter over time. Opt to invest in a nice reusable grocery bag that you can use over and over again.

Junk drawers: We all have that one drawer that we only use for the storage of 'random junk': from coins, small candles, scissors measuring tapes to rubber bands. Although this drawer is very convenient, it often accumulates stuff that can be eliminated.

You will find that half the stuff in the junk drawer is in fact things that you never use or need. Unfortunately, the few important items in the junk drawer are difficult to locate because of the disorganized array. Sort out the items and discard all that can be considered as trash.

It will be wise to make use of clear glass jars and airtight containers to keep the small items more organized.

Sort the kitchen linens: I am convinced that you won't wear ratty and torn undies hidden beneath your clothes. Right? Why should you then have dingy and torn dish towels and rags on display in your kitchen? If I were to visit your home and happened to see the nasty dish rags you use to wash and wipe the dishes, I will certainly not eat at your home -no matter how much of a foodie I am. If you desire a kitchen with a hygienic appearance, throw out all the torn and stained towels.

Breakables: It is advisable that you immediately ditch any chipped, broken or cracked crockery. They are not only unsightly, but also unhealthy and dangerous. Besides being the ideal nesting place for bacteria, items with chips and cracks can easily break during heating or cooling. No time for second thoughts here - just bin them!

Upper Cabinets vs. Lower Cabinets

For a clutter-free kitchen and for items to be within easy reach, it is important to have your upper and lower cabinets well organized.

Lower cabinets closests to the cooker are the most suitable storage spot for pots, pans and other cookware. To maximize storage space, it is advisable to store pans on their sided and pots nested together. It will be sensible to invest in a pull out organizer for installment in the cabinets for better organization of the pans and lids. Frequently used kitchen appliances should be moved to the countertop for ease of access during food preparation. However, if your counter space is limited, place them on the lower cabinets just below the main work area. Appliances that are not used frequently should also be stored on the lower cabinets.

Store cleaning supplies and pet products under the sink cabinet and be sure to use a lock - especially if you have kids or pets at home. Cluttering of this cabinet can be avoided by installing hooks or a cabinet door rack for the hanging of brushes, rags and rubber gloves.

The most convenient place for breakables like glassware and dishes, are the upper cabinets. Consider placing these dishes in the cabinet directly over the dishwasher or drying rack for convenience when unloading.

If you do not have a pantry, you can also store foodstuffs in the upper cabinets. Store the spices, bottles, food storage containers and other food items on the cabinets above your kitchen work station. Just remember to keep the labels facing towards the front and to keep similar items lined up together.

Cookbooks can be stored in the hard to reach shelves, as you'll probably not use them very often. However, make sure that you throw out the cookbooks with outdated recipes and the ones that you have never used.

Plastics and other glass storage containers can be placed right above the counter space you use to containerize leftovers or bulk purchases like cereals, sugar and flour.

NB: Below is an illustration as guideline to achieve and organized and clutter-free kitchen cabinets.

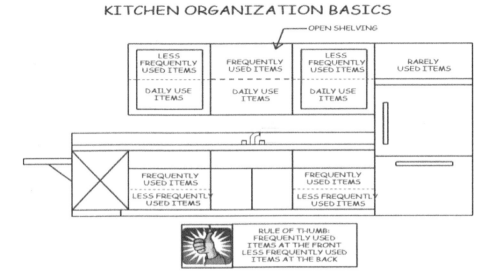

KITCHEN ORGANIZATION BASICS

2. The Countertop

Kitchen countertops are prone to be the most cluttered place, being the general storage area all sorts of stuff. You name it and you will find it there: anything from fresh produce, appliance chargers, keys, loose change, empty cans, papers, cookware, appliances, etc. Although we think these things belong on the countertop, they are in fact the perfect example of **clutter**!

Here is a guide that will show you the way to a sacred countertop that is clutter-free.

Appliances: As discussed in the cabinets section, appliances that are not used daily, should not be on the countertop. There is no need for a bread maker or food processor sitting on the countertop and you only use it a few times a week. Create more space on the counter and store them in the lower cabinets.

If you have a very small kitchen, you might consider to store the appliances used daily in a handy cabinet just below the counter to keep your countertop clutter-free.

Keys: When family members enter the house, they often place keys on the countertop. Keys lying around can cause a cluttered appearance, especially if you have a large family. The trick is to keep a specific bowl for keys or to install a wall rack for hanging of the keys.

Cookbooks: We earlier suggested that you can keep cookbooks in the upper cabinets. If you however use your cookbooks quite often, you can consider storing them in a basket in the cabinet just below the counter. Better still, take photos on your phone of your favorite recipes and ditch the cookbooks - especially if limited space is one of your concerns.

Bills, mails and paper: Invest in an over-the-door pocket organizer for all the important bills after you have sorted them. The best way to manage your mail, is to sort it as soon as it arrives at your home. Trash the junk mail and then file the rest. As for paper, sort it out. Shred and trash what is junk, but identify a perfect spot for the filing of the useful papers.

The drying rack: Chances are good that you allow the utensils to dry on the drying rack before they get stored in the cabinets. Instead of keeping the rack on the countertop, consider putting it in the sink area. Better still, let your dishes dry in the dishwasher. If you hand wash your dishes, consider immediately drying the utensils with a kitchen towel, rather than having them sit on the countertop.

Purses, schoolbooks and backpacks: You need to start a re-education program by announcing to all family members that your kitchen is now sacred and a clutter-free zone. Make it known to all family members that purses, wallets, briefcases and books are no longer allowed on the kitchen counters. Instead, get them involved in inventing creative and alternative ideas for the organized storage of stuff.

TIP: Get into the habit of cleaning the countertops every night before retiring to bed. This way, you will always wake up energized and thrilled to find a clean and clutter-free countertop.

3. The Refrigerator

The refrigerator is often crammed with lots of food, jars and bottles that can result in messy drips, spills and crusty junk. To keep it clean, organized and clutter-free can therefore be a very daunting task.

However, I will guide you through this process to make it easier for you.

Start off by removing all the content from the refrigerator and place it on the counter. Thoroughly clean the shelves and the fridge walls with soap, warm water and a small scrub brush.

Check the expiry dates of all the items you removed from the refrigerator. Make sure that you trash every item that has expired and do the same with food leftovers that you've kept for longer than four days.

Wipe any containers that have drip marks on them before you return them to the refrigerator.

Clean every other shelf, drawer and bin in the refrigerator. During the cleaning process, make notes of any storage items or food products that needs to be on your shopping list.

Wear your rubber gloves and head to the freezer compartment. The gloves will help protect your hands from numbing. Remove the food in the freezer and place it on the counter. If the cleaning process is going to take longer than 15 minutes, it is desirable to transfer the food on the counter to a cooler to avoid thawing and spoiling. Make sure that you get rid of any item that might appear stale. Restock everything else as soon as you're done with the cleaning of the freezer.

The next step is to thoroughly clean the outside of the refrigerator as well as the top of the unit. If there is clutter on top of the fridge - like school papers, old photos and drawings - discard them or store them in an appropriate place.

Refrigerator Organizing Tips

- If you come across duplicate items such as soy sauce, olive oil or ketchup, combine them in a single bottle. But make sure to check expiration dates; you don't want to combine fresh items with items that have already expired.

- Avoid storing unopened and nonperishables like sodas in the refrigerator. Rather store them in the pantry to maximize your fridge space.
- Freeze milk, cheese and meats to save space in the refrigerator compartment.
- Store food in clear containers to make it easy to see the contents when necessary.
- Pat dry your fruits and vegetables before storage to get rid of extra moisture.
- Don't let the 'Best Before" date confuse you. It only applies to unopened food. Make a note of the date that you open the food, as this will prevent you from eating stale and spoilt food.

4. The Pantry

Just like cabinets, the pantry is often cluttered because it serves as a storage area. In fact, after cleaning the cabinets, countertops and the refrigerator, chances are that you have transferred quite a bulk to the pantry.

This area is often neglected, because the door always stay closed and we only open when we need to get a particular item in there.

But why should your pantry always scream for attention?

Start off by removing everything from the pantry. Then take your cleaning supplies and scrub down the pantry. Although pantries accumulate a lot of dirt, they rarely get the attention they need. Now that you've made the time and have an empty pantry, do a thorough cleaning and pay close attention to the walls, shelves and the floor.

Next, take a look at all the stuff you removed from the shelves and determine the value of each and every item. Ask yourself the following three questions.

1. Is this item taking up too much valuable space?
2. Do we frequently use this item?
3. Is it an item we only use on special occasions?

Get rid of anything you don't use. For items used infrequently, move them to the highest shelf. Food and other supplies used on a daily basis, should be placed within reach.

Pantry Organizing Tips

- Group similar items together to find them quickly and for ease of retrieving them, for example, coffee supplies together, all cans together, spices together, etc.
- An assortment of clear plastic or glass containers can help you store and seal foods like cereals, pasta, snacks, etc. Airtight containers will also protect your food-stuffs from dust and pests invasion.
- If you have a small pantry, make use of wall and floor space. For instance, you can use wall organizers, tiered racks or hooks for spice storage, aprons, towels, etc. Baskets and bins can also go a long way to provide more storage possibilities. The point is, be creative in obtaining as much space as possible. You already know that space is a valuable commodity. Don't you?
- If your pantry is large, use the pantry to store small appliances, bulk water and other items that might be crowding other rooms. Just be careful not to leave it cluttered.
- You can use a label marker on containers and bins for ease of reference.
- If you use plastic grocery bags, consider getting a bin to keep them orderly and organized.
- In case you have kids, create a snacking zone. Place the snacks on an easy to reach spot so that they can easily be grabbed after school or when necessary.

Decluttering the Living Room

After the kitchen, the living room is the second most cluttered area in most homes. This is where we gather to watch TV, play games, sit and chat as a family, entertain our visitors and a place where we can put our feet up and relax. Everyone therefore craves for a spacious living room that can easily accommodate all the above needs.

The living room is visible and you can't prevent visitors from accessing it. That's why a friend will call to inform you that he/she is visiting and in a spark of a minute you will embark on clearing every visible clutter in your living room.

Crammed tables, exposed cable wires, rumpled blankets, unrelated items on the fireplace mantle and objects strewn on the coffee table are some of the things that make a living room cluttered.

To give back life to your sitting room, this is the steps to follow.

Tame the technology

Given that the living room is an entertainment centre, the temptation to have all sorts of tech gadgets there is real. If you can't keep your hands off these gadgets, invest in a TV cupboard with storage drawers to keep them organized. It will prevent the lying around of remote controls, DVDs and game consoles across every surface.

Put up shelves

A good looking open shelf can be a great investment for displaying some of those favorite decor items. On these shelves, you can also place pretty document holders to keep magazines organized.

Be imaginative with your storage ideas

Do you have odd woven baskets tucked away in the store? Revamp them as part of your living room essentials. These baskets do not only add a touch of class to the room, but also serve as storage for stuff you are not ready to discard yet. Such can include books, magazines and toys.

Living Room Organizing Tips

- If your home needs a makeover, consider purchasing furniture that has storage space. This can be the coffee table, the couch and sofas. The extra space will go a long way to help eliminate stuff getting scattered across the room.
- Do you love watching movies and listening to movies? Does it bother you to always have several compact discs lying flat on the TV cabinet? Instead of the traditional CDs and DVDs, why don't you consider digital versions of movies and music. Through services such as Hulu and Netflix, you can stream live through your TV and be entertained all day long - all clutter-free.
- Since the living room is a common area for the family, everyone should be incorporated in decluttering and keeping it organized. Get the opinion and feedback of everyone regarding the appearance of the room, instead of making unilateral decisions. This way, every family member will always contribute towards keeping the room a clutter-free zone.

Decluttering the Bedrooms

The most exciting thing about bedrooms is how we keep them behind key and lock with the hope that no one can access them.

It rarely goes about privacy and the hiding of boxes of money and jewelry in there, but mostly involves the clutter we often tuck away in that room.

Compared to the kitchen and living room, bedrooms are 'less visible' and therefore, are often neglected. We often hop out of bed, simply leaving the bed unmade and blankets in a tangle. Clothes are strewn across the room, laundry is piled up and plenty of unnecessary items get stuffed under the bed. It's time we reclaimed our bedrooms and got them back on the prioritized visibility scale.

The Master Bedroom

Your master bedroom should be inviting, tranquil and useful.

Creating the perfect ambience in this room will not only help you sleep better, but will also improve your sex life, privacy and mental health.

To give your master bedroom an overall cleansing and leave it clutter-free, you'll need your partner's participation. This is because the stuff in the room belong to both of you and you possibly can't decide on their behalf which items to keep, toss or donate.

The Basic Bedroom Clutter

As stated above, your bedroom is likely to accumulate all sorts of stuff that you possibly don't need: from dishes, papers, books and stuff that do not belong there.

Sort everything out and move everything where it belongs - clean clothes in the closet; dirty clothes in the laundry room; dirty dishes in the dishwasher; stuff that you don't need in the trash bin, etc.

When sorting the clothes, check on those that you no longer wear and put them in an appropriate box awaiting donation.

For the important papers, books and magazines, file them or put them in a storage box. However, be sure to trash old magazines that are already outdated. You should actually consider subscribing to online magazines, as this will nip in the bud most of your home clutter.

This is the same case with old books. Printed books take up plenty of unnecessary space. Opting to read Kindle books and eBooks can go a long way in minimizing clutter in the bedroom. Therefore just pare a few of your favorite reads and no matter how hard it is, donate and discard the rest.

Under the bed

When did you last check what is under your bed? This is often the perfect spot to accumulate all sorts of clutter. As a rule, we keep various types of unnecessary junk under the bed, hoping that this will make the bedroom appear more organized. On the contrary, we end up creating a messy, untidy and sometimes smelly bedroom.

Start off by neatly making your bed. Next, pull out everything under the bed and sort through the items. Group them into things you would like to keep, discard, give away or donate.

Try to keep the area under your bed a completely clutter-free zone. Your bed should serve its purpose as your sleeping area and not as a hiding place for unnecessary stuff.

However, if you're truly short of space, you can use an under bed storage basket or container for storage of seasonal clothing and bedding. Even then, it's advisable to use plastic bins instead of wood, cardboard and canvas. Plastic offers better protection against dust and bed bugs compared to the other materials.

You can use a bed skirt to cover the space between the bed and floor if you do not want the boxes exposed.

Bedroom Furniture

Dressers, bookcases, linen chests and bedside tables can easily become a hub for the storage of random items: buttons, coins and keys among other things.

Start off by dusting these surfaces and replace the bedside lamp and telephone if need be. Concerning small random items, put them in a zippered bag if you still find them useful.

If you fancy nicely framed photos, opt to use only a few favorite ones instead of cluttering your tables. The rest of the photos can be hung against the wall in a stylish and decorative way.

To ensure the bedroom is not always cluttered with tiny random items, place a decorative bowl on the table or chest and use it for the storage of coins, nail clippers and other pocket items.

Always remember that less is more. The more organized the bedroom surfaces are, the better and more comfortable you will feel in that room. Cluttered furniture creates distraction and anxiety.

Drawers

We keep undies, pajamas, T-shirts, sweaters and random items in the drawers. To thoroughly declutter the drawers, you'll need your partner's participation to prevent throwing out things that he/she considers as valuable.

Remove everything, clean the surfaces and use a drawer liner if need be. Start sorting the items and organize them into groups of four; what to toss, what to keep, what to keep elsewhere and what to donate.

Discard anything that is old, tattered, permanently stained, missing a partner (eg. socks), no longer fits or never ever been worn.

In the drawers, group together similar items; for instance, under pants together, bras in the same drawer, hosiery and tights together, etc. You can also sort them by color or utility if space is not a problem.

If you're short of space, consider hanging jeans and khakis on hangers instead of folding them and storing them in drawers. Keep in mind that sweaters and knitwear should never be hung, but rather folded. This is where a deep drawer comes in handy.

Take notes of any organizers or drawer dividers that you might need to purchase to keep everything tidy and organized.

Finally, give the entire room a thorough final cleaning. Vacuum the floor and the curtains, whilst not forgetting to wipe the window sills and picture frames.

Once you're satisfied with the appearance of the room, take a photo of it to remind you how beautiful a decluttered and clean bedroom is.

Kids' Bedroom

Your kids' rooms can often feel and appear like a war zone with toys, clothes, crafts and books strewn across the room. It's even worse if the little humans never bother to keep their rooms tidy.

But all is not over, you can keep the rooms clutter-free without restricting your kids from playing in their rooms.

But how?

Toys

We always want the best for our kids, but we often end up giving them more than they simply to prove our love to them. It is very likely that your children have more toys than they will ever need.

In a research conducted by Claire Lerner, she stated that giving children too many toys or the wrong type of toys can harm them. Kids become overwhelmed easily, making it difficult to concentrate long enough on a single thing. Other psychologists have also indicated that too many toys distract children and prevent them from learning and playing well.

Now is the perfect time to cut down on all the toys flooding your kids' rooms. Keep just a few toys that are age appropriate and the toys that promote problem-solving, creativity and social interaction skills.

Cutting down on toys also helps reduce sibling rivalry and can teach kids valuable lessons, such as sharing with other needy kids and being mindful about spending.

So, where do we start?

Talk to your kids and let them know that they have more than enough toys. Ask them to select their favorite toys that they would love to keep. Have an intense discussion and let your kids know how grateful other needy kids would be to enjoy the toys they have outgrown. Give them freedom to decide who they would love to gift or donate to. You'll be surprised to find that kids are very compassionate and more than willing to give and share.

Organize the toys they would like to keep in a basket or shelves for easy access. Be sure to disinfect them beforehand to avoid spreading of germs to family members.

If there are any broken toys or missing important pieces, toss them in the garbage bin.

Books

Start off by dividing the books into two groups: one group for the books they still read and the other group for books they have either outgrown or simply don't like. For the latter, just donate them. Resist any temptation of keeping the books to read to your grandchildren someday. Sometimes it's not worth it.

Make sure to neatly organize the books that are still in use on easy accessible shelves or in neat storage baskets. And remember to lay down strict rules for where books should be stored after use.

Art works

Discarding your kids' beautiful arts and crafts can be very difficult. You'd rather keep their favorite arts safely to show it to them when they have grown up. Indeed, they are cherished keepsakes.

But what do you do if they are cluttering the kids' rooms?

Let your kids' identify the most important art works they would like to keep. This can be handprints, special notes and some of their best artworks. Help them with the selection process, lest they get attached to all the crafts.

As for everything else, help your kids with the discarding process.

It is important to create a display area in their room where only the meaningful creations can get pinned and displayed.

Decluttering the Laundry Room

The laundry room is often the most unutilized room in the home. For this reason it accumulates a lot of junk, ranging from piles of dirty clothes, smelly shoes, pet food and other random items. It can be best referred to as the junk drawer in most homes.

But this needs improvement! Your laundry room needs to look, feel and smell fresh. Nothing feels as good as walking into a clean, organized and clutter-free laundry room.

Start off by folding any clothes that could still be in the dryer or the laundry basket. Next, remove anything that could be on top of the washer and dryer. Thoroughly clean these surfaces, paying attention to the top, outside and the crevices where debris accumulates. Also make sure to clean the knobs and the lint filter.

Once you're done cleaning the machines, you'll need to focus on the storage spaces; storage bins, open shelves, laundry baskets and the drying racks.

Remove items on the shelves, wipe clean and add a shelf liner if necessary. Sort the items you have removed and group them into four piles: what to return to the shelves, what to keep elsewhere, what to give away and what to discard. Don't forget to remove any items stuck in cabinets and behind the door.

Laundry Room Organizing Tips

Consider purchasing a mop and broom holder that can be mounted behind the door. Stacking them against the wall, does not only create disarray but also makes it unsightly.

Use baskets and plastic bins for the storage of random items in the laundry room. Cleaning supplies should be in one bin - detergents, bleach and fabric softener in another. If you store pet items in the laundry room, keep food and other pet stuff in a separate container.

If you are short of space, consider purchasing a shelving tower that can be used to store extra baskets and storage bins.

To keep everything organized, categorize the shelves according to their function. This will make it easy to find and grab things and will make chores quicker to complete.

Decluttering the Bathrooms

Bathrooms are busy rooms. Bathing, showering and grooming by multiple users are daily activities that make it tough to prevent bathroom clutter.

Bathrooms require ample storage space for all the grooming tools we use on a daily basis. Unfortunately, most bathrooms have limited space than can easily cause cluttering. Despite the compactness of your bathroom, you can still organize it properly. You'll be surprised to discover that most of the stuff that crowds your bathroom space is unused and unnecessary. The space might appear bigger if you can manage to sort similar items together. Try to keep different categories separated from each other: cosmetics, skin care essentials, shaving supplies, nair care items and hair accessories.

For shared bathrooms, consider designating individual drawers, shelves and baskets for the users. You should however take extra caution in shared bathrooms. Let it be known what can be shared and what not to. Cosmetics, toothbrushes and hairbrushes should never be shared to prevent the spread of infections. However, toiletries, shampoo, lotion, toothpaste and facial cleansers can always be shared.

So, how do you go about the decluttering of these items?

Towels

Are all your towels in good shape? For towels that have been used for ages, use them as rags. If they are still in a usable condition, you can donate them to an animal shelter. You however need to limit the number of towels you have in the bathroom to prevent an overfull appearance. Two towels per family member are enough. You can keep a few extra towels for the rare times you have guests or visitors.

Wrong shades that you bought by accident, should preferably be discarded or donated. Old makeup and empty bottles should be thrown away. If you want to make sure that your makeup is still in a good condition, simply check the following rules:

- Mascara and liquid eyeliner should be replaced after every three to four months
- When kept in a cool and dry place, liquid foundation can last up to a year
- Lipsticks and lipgloss can be used for a year and six months respectively
- When kept away from moisture, beauty powders can safely be kept for up to two years
- Throw out all brushes that are already losing fibers. If you only use 2-3 brushes in a set of 10, consider giving away the others instead of filling up your drawers. Clean the brushes that you use regularly properly before you return them to the drawer.

Hair Products and Accessories

Any hair product that never worked for you should be trashed. Old products and the ones you regret buying, should also be put away. All air accessories like ties, headbands and elastics should be organized together and the items you no longer wear should be ditched. Toss hair brushes and combs that you don't use and clean what you would like to keep.

Skin Products

Just like the hair products, dispose of those that are old and that doesn't work for you.

Nail Care Supplies

Although nail polish can last for years if kept out of direct sunlight, always look for changes such as clumpiness and then opt to rather throw it away. However, you don't have to wait until it goes bad. If you don't use it or don't like the color, give it away. For other nail accessories like clippers, polish remover and files, put them in a small make-up-tote to prevent them from cluttering the drawers.

Beauty Appliances

Evaluate whether you still need the hair dryers, straighteners, shavers, foot baths and other appliances that you possess. You could be holding onto one of those items, hoping to use them 'someday'. If you haven't used something for the last six months, that 'someday' will never come.

What is the point of keeping a foot bath that you only use once a year? You'd rather opt to get rid of it and head to a beauty salon for a pedicure.

Bath Toys

Bath toys are great for small kids. However, too many of them become junk that can cluter your bathroom. Sort them out and discard worn toys or the ones that have grown mold on them. For those outgrown by your kids, consider gifting them to needy kids.

Medication

Most of us love storing medicine in the bathroom. This is not at all advisable! Besides the temperature fluctuations in the bathroom, children can easily get hold of the medicine which makes it very hazardous. Collect all the medicines and safely dispose of those that have expired or are no longer used. Consider getting an ideal storage cabinet for the medication (A locked cabinet in the kitchen will be fine). However, your first aid supplies can be kept in the bathroom and can include thermometers, bandages, adhesive tape, syringes etc.

Let's now take a look at the various areas to pay attention to when organizing your bathroom.

Bathroom Surfaces

These include the sink, the tub, toilet area, countertop and the cabinets. You can start off with the area around the sink. Remove everything around that area, such as toothbrushes, toothpaste, soap, etc. Give the sink a thorough cleaning whilst paying close attention to the counter space, mirror and faucet.

Once done, restock the items you removed, but remember to throw away anything you consider as clutter. Ensure the toothbrushes are in a neat container and kept upright to dry out.

In most cases, the counter space is the prime real estate in bathrooms. Try to keep the countertop as clutter-free as possible. The only items that should be kept there are your daily cologne, hand soap and lotion. Limit decorative items on the countertop to prevent cluttering.

If you use the tub regularly, a wall organizer or decorative shelf will be extremely practical for the storage of body wash and other bathing necessities.

If you like reading in the bathroom, a combo toilet paper holder and magazine holder can help to keep your favorite reading material close at hand and organized.

The Shower

Remove all the bottles, razors, soaps and cleansers from the shower cubicle. Give the shower and the shower door a thorough cleaning. Sort through the items and discard any rusty razors, soap scraps and empty bottles. Make sure to wipe clean all the other bottles you'll be returning to the shower. They often accumulate excess gunk on the outside that makes them unsightly.

You can consider investing in a mountable dispenser unit if you're tired of so many bottles in the shower. With the dispenser unit, you can conveniently pump out the desired amount of shampoo, conditioner and soap.

Under the Sink

Just like the under sink cabinet in the kitchen, this area in the bathroom is often also a cluttered and disorganized zone. Remove everything underneath the sink and clean the area. It is always a brilliant idea to line the area with a waterproof shelf liner.

Sort out all the items, and throw out all the expired supplies, torn rags and everything else that appears to be clutter. Make sure that you move items that do not belong in the under sink cabinet. Put them in their rightful place. Remember to put anything that you might want to give away in the donation box.

A wire rack or an organizer mounted on the cabinet door can help you to keep any bottles or random items under the sink organized. Pull out shelves are also a great way to keep everything neat. If you do not have the above items, note them down in a notebook and consider purchasing them on your next shopping spree.

Better still, use stackable baskets to keep the under sink items organized. It will be practical to group similar items together for ease of access.

In case you have a pedestal sink, make use of a storage tower or drawer units. You can get some awesome ideas on Pinterest.

Decluttering Closets and Clothes

When closing your closet door becomes a war, it's time to get rid of some items in the closet. Having a spacious and organized closet might seem like a magical dream to most of us. Some of us tend to think that a full closet gives us a sense of emotional fulfillment. Well, your closet might be full, but you only use 30% of the items in the closet. Does this make sense to you?

But come to think of it... why do we keep clothing that we no longer wear?

Guilt: You've spent a lot of money to buy that grey cardigan that didn't fit, right? Or what about that dress you received from your BFF, but isn't really your style? Never feel guilty to let go of such clothing! Their presence in your closet only makes you feel bad and adds no value to your well-being. The scenario will immediately change if you donate them to someone who needs them and who can wear and use them.

The desire to look different: The shape of your body has changed over the years. You have given birth, have no time for workouts and stress has changed your body size. Some clothes are now too small and don't fit you any longer. You're however in denial and keep hoping that, 'someday' you'll get back into shapeand that you will be able to reclaim the clothes. But will that 'someday' ever come? Get rid of the unused clothes and, if you ever get back your perfect body, you'll be in the position to get a few newer and nicer trends.

I'll need it someday: This imaginative 'someday' will probably never come and if it does, it shall be too late. If you haven't worn clothes for the past one or two years, the odds are you'll never wear it again. Your preferences will also change over time and you might find that your unused clothes don't interest you any-more. So, live in the present and forget the 'someday' phrase.

How to tackle decluttering

Just like in the previous sections, get ready with some bins. Four bins are enough.

- One bin for clothes you use, need and love.
- A second bin for clothing that you love but that need repairs; like hemming, mending, buttons, etc. Never return these items to the closet unless they have been repaired.
- The third bin should specifically be for trash. Torn and unmendable items and clothes that are out of style belong in this bin.
- The fourth bin is for donations. This bin is for lightly used clothes that are still in perfect condition. You can also choose to sell them off, but this might take some time and energy.

Remove everything from your closets. Yes, every little thing - clothes, shoes, accessories, etc. Remember to include items that could still be in the laundry.

If possible, try on most of the things and take a good look at your-self in front of the mirror. If you're lucky to have a loyal friend, count on her advise as to what you need to let go. Only keep items that fit you and have a useful purpose in your life. If you want to feel confident in your clothing, only keep clothing that you really like. During your trying on session, sort out the clothes and sort them into the respective bins.

Decluttering the Kids' Clothes

Compared to adults, children grow out of their clothes quite fast. It is hence most likely that you are stuck with plenty of kiddies' clothes that is not in use any longer.

Empty out the entire closet and drawers and go through every item of clothing. If your kids are around, you can let them try on some of the clothes to determine if the clothes still fit. If they are present, they can help you to make the final choice regarding the keeping or discarding of some clothing. Keep in mind that kids can be quite picky at times! If the kids are not present, as sizing reference you can use a set of clothes you are sure fit them perfectly well.

If you end up with a lot of brand clothing that is still in perfect condition, consider selling the clothes. However, be sure that it's worth your time and money, since the returns can be quite small.

Closet and Clothing Organizing Tips

- Consider getting a hanging shoe rack or an over the door organizer to avoid overcrowding in the closet.
- Make it a family affair. Let everyone join in and help to organize the clothing. This should not be a one day affair but a daily challenge to every family member.
- Schedule an hour per week to keep the closets in perfect order. This will prevent clutter build up.
- For items you use infrequently, such as hats, purses, ties, suitcases, etc., store them on the highest shelves. Items you use regularly need to be stored within easy reach.
- Organize clothes for different seasons on different hangers. For instance, summer clothes can be stored on yellow hangers, red hangers can be used for fall clothing, white hangers can be used for winter clothes and green hangers for

spring clothes. Just be creative. If your space is limited, store off season clothing in vacuum storage bags or decorative baskets with bins which can easily transition as furniture.

- You can use a handbag organizer on the closet shelf to keep all your bags and purses on display.
- Random items that are of no value should be trashed.
- Once all is organized and orderly, applaud yourself for a great job well done. Treat yourself to a salon pedicure or buy yourself that silk shirt you've been eyeing for such a long time. You deserve it!

Decluttering the Office/Study Room

The study room can become a mess if you work from home or the kids do their homework there. If not careful, the room can easily become a dumping ground for unnecessary items such as cardboards for kids' projects, mirrors and old pictures mounted on the walls. A disorganized home office can lead to the loss of important documents and a lot of time wastage while trying to look for essential objects.

This being your home office, should be managed in a professional way. Only keep items related to your business and things that will improve your productiveness.

It doesn't matter how large or small your office is. The decluttering process possibly remains the same - filing of paperwork, storage for supplies and organizing the work station.

Let's see how we can declutter the office on an area by area basis.

The work station

Your work station is the office desk. It is similar to the countertop in the kitchen.

Start off by getting everything off the desk and wipe clean the surface. Once everything is out of the way, it becomes easy to organize the area.

As you start restocking, the only stuff that should be on the desk are the items you use on a daily basis. This includes your computer and its accessories, a stapler, a pen (not an assortment), paper and the table calendar. These items should be within arms reach when you're seated.

If the office desk is quite big, you can consider placing a framed photo or a decorative item on the desk. However, be careful not to overload this space.

Paperwork can easily clutter the desk if caution is not taken. Decide how to discard of the 'not so important' papers before they become a pain in the office. For the important notes, be sure to file them.

The printer and scanner do not belong on the desk. Besides being bulky, they are not used every day. You can get a place underneath the desk or a convenient place within the room, and place them there.

Electronics

As you declutter the office desk, clean up all the electronics with a lint free rag: from the monitor, keyboard, phone, printers, scanners, photocopier and any other electronic that could be in the room. Use an LCD cleaning solution to clean the screens to avoid damage or leaving streaks.

You should however make it a weekly task to clean up the electronics. They easily accumulate dust which can be a health risk.

Drawers

The desk drawers are often the prime real estate for all the junk that has been cleared off the office desk. The only way to avoid a disorganized mess, is to store similar items together or frequently used items in the same drawer. For instance, office supplies used regularly, such as pencils, paper clips, scissors, etc., should be kept next to each other.

Make use of plastic or cardboard inserts to segregate the various items in a drawer. You can get even more creative and use cans, mason jars and egg cartons for better organization.

Reorganize your drawers after every 30 days to ensure that all junk is kept at bay.

Paperwork

As mentioned above, paperwork is a necessary evil that you can't avoid in your office. You might decide to go paperless, but that is still not a solution. You'll always need to scan and file these digital files.

The solution is to deal with paperwork as soon as it gets into the office. Create a filing system that allows you to take action relating to all the paperwork you receive every day.

Sort the papers according to the actions that need to be taken. For instance, the paperwork that requires immediate attention, should go in one tray, bills go into another and archived paperwork into another. By the end of the day, all paperwork received on that day should have been acted upon: important paperwork should be stored, sent to recipients and the unimportant paperwork should be destroyed.

You should also consider filing the papers in multicolored files based on the action that needs to be taken. For instance, you can have a folder for read and sign, bills, make calls, write back, etc. Organizing them in separate folders, will help to quickly identify any uncompleted tasks.

Designate an area in the office where you can keep the files folders and file boxes. Since the world is adversely going paperless, a single cabinet or drawer should be sufficient for the storage of the filing system.

However, don't file every single paper that you come across. Destroy and shred any documents with personal information.

As the paperwork accumulates and the single cabinet becomes short of space, you will have to come up with plan **B**. Use a high speed scanner to keep the 'not so import' paperwork in digital form. For the most valuable paperwork like legal and tax documents, always keep them in printed form (you can however scan a copy for digital purposes).

Cables and cords

Your office has several electronics which each comes with cables and cords. If not careful, this can cause a cluttered office space and worst of all, it can cause accidents. Invest in zip ties to secure the cables and prevent trip accidents. You can also label the cords to help you identify the specific cord you are looking for.

Decluttering the Basement and the Garage

Kitchen goods, lawn and gardening equipment, power tools, seasonal decorations and various unused items are often kept in the basement or the garage. These two places are often treated like a dumping ground for stuff that should otherwise be eliminated. Although we sometimes keep stuff here with the intention of using them later, clutter accumulates over time making the area quite unsightly.

Like all the other decluttering projects, start off by pulling everything out. Give the inside of your garage or basement a thorough, deserving and proper cleaning. Remove cobwebs, sweep every corner, empty the flower pots if any, and clean all the dirty surfaces.

Sort everything into two piles; one pile for the things you'll keep and the other pile for things you'll discard. You already know the rule of the thumb; if you haven't used it for a year or two, it's time to let go!

When done, clean the items you intend to restock in the garage. Ones they are all clean, start returning them by grouping similar items together. This will make it easier to find items when necessary.

Remember that Decluttering the garage or basement might require lifting of heavy items. Ask a friend or family members to help you out.

If you keep a lot of athletic gear and equipments in the basement, consider installing racks and shelves to keep everything organized.

Understand what to keep and not to keep in this area. Paint should not be stored in the garage because of its hazardous nature, instead drop it off at a waste plant. Also avoid storing canned food, gas grills and electronics in the basement due to lack of ventilation and the extreme temperatures.

CHAPTER 3. GETTING EVERYONE ABOARD

N ow that you have decluttered almost every spot in your home, the odds are that you already hate clutter. You have come to realize how clutter can be a pain in the butt, cause you unnecessary stress and worst of all never allow you comfort in your own home.

It's now time to help others delight in the goodness of this journey. These people will possibly never beg you to help them declutter. However, the fact that you have been reading this book and made up your mind to detox your home, shows how much you care about decluttering.

Your friends, children, relatives and even spouse all have clutter in their lives. They are tired of it and want it wiped out. But they don't know how to tackle it hands on!

How do you make your appearance in and become their guardian angel?

How do you apply the knowledge you gained from this book and from the physical decluttering of your own home?

This is what we are going to discuss in this chapter.

What kind of help will you offer?

The kind of assistance you offer will depend on two aspects. One: the prospect asked for your help to declutter. Two: the person you intend to help has not asked for your help. However, you have to declutter the place, as the space belongs to you or you have a say in that space.

Regarding those who've ask for your help, it's pretty easy. You were invited because they believe that your contribution is valuable. You can confidently share ideas and the person will gladly consider your suggestions to help eliminate clutter.

On the other hand, if you haven't been invited to declutter, it can be a bit difficult but still not impossible. You'll need to prove that you truly can pull it off. Earn their credibility by decluttering your own place first. Make visible progress before you attempt to convince them to tidy up their homes.

For instance, it is logical to first get rid of your own clutter before telling your mother in law that you'll be coming over to declutter her home?

Thumb rules when helping out

1. Go with your prospect's instincts

Give the person you're helping out the freedom to follow their own heart. Allow them to decide what they'd like to keep or donate and let them come up with the best suggestions where to put things. Don't dictate but rather be the muscle and brain behind the decluttering project. Give ideas but allow them to either adopt or disregard them. Remember, it's their space and they are the ones who'll be responsible for maintaining it after you've left. However, help them to trust their own instincts.

2. Don't leave them with a bigger mess

You have already learnt in this book how to declutter without leaving a place messy. You also already know how to manage clutter after you've identified it. Use these same strategies when helping a friend. Don't let them remove everything from the closet and then leave them on there own because you are going to look for your cat that is missing. You'll not only leave your friend with a bigger mess, but he/she will never accept your help again.

3. Be professional

You might not be a professional declutterer, but you must be accommodating and kind to the person you are helping. Control your tongue and avoid getting too personal. The fact that they allowed you into their home is enough to respect their privacy and treat them with respect.

Helping Friends

We love our friends. We laugh, hang out, dine together and fight every now and them. But still, we solve our problems and get back together, simply because we adore them.

If you'll be helping your friend to declutter, then focus on the decluttering and nothing else. You'll be tempted to chat or go out and postpone the project for another day. Please avoid this scenario. Don't be distracted by the hot gossip burning your throat. You're there to help him/her live a clutter-free life.

You are the person who must keep your friend focused and prevent thoughts of 'prostasticlutter' from popping up in her mind. When your friend sees how motivated you are, he/she will have no option but to follow suit.

Build trust

Clutter is intensely personal of nature. Build trust by listening to your friend's concerns instead of condemning them. Don't roll your eyes if your friend keeps jewelry on the living room coffee table. Just smile and help her find a better place. For your friend to become a declutterer, he/she needs to be accepted for who and for the way they are. If you judge him/her, they will try to defend their way of life and why they still need to live the way they are - even when it is very clear that their current life is disastrous. Ask the various decluttering questions we've discussed earlier on. Be keen to read his/her mind to determine whether he/she is making up answers to impress you. Encourage him/her to be honest in order to provide a solution to a problem. If in doubt of your decluttering method, explain why those decluttering questions are of importance.

Celebrate the small milestones as you progress

Praise the visible progress the two of you are making. It will encourage your friend and provide the motivation and strength to get going. As there is a consistent decrease in the volume of clutter, volume of clutter, there might even be an improvement in answering the various decluttering questions.

Embrace the finishing together

When completing the decluttering project, exhaustion and distractions will definitely show up. Your friend might not have the strength to get to the tip of the iceberg, but you are her supporting muscle. Stay focused amidst the fatigue, as this will continually inspire your friend to the very end.

Help your friend maintain the decluttered home

Don't be the threatening friend. Paying your friend unexpected visits to scrutinize his/her cluttering habits, is going to ruin the issue. That's not what a decluttering helper does. Of course the reappearance of clutter will worry and upset you, but don't give up. As a true friend, offer your help again and don't grow weary from asking the same questions over and over again.

In the long run your friend will get to trust you even more, since you'll have an understanding of how his/her home works. And finally the beauty and bliss of decluttering will be evident and applauded!

Lastly, try to encourage your friend to look for other friends that they can help with decluttering too.

Helping kids

Decluttering with kids can be a challenge, especially if they don't understand what clutter really is. But working with them is fun and quite enjoyable. The fact that they are the children and you are the grown up is the greatest advantage. They'll easily take orders and leave you in charge to give guidance and direction.

You will most likely be helping them to clean up their play area. The play area could be a separate playroom or their own bedrooms. These rooms often become a storage place for toys instead of a playing area. It can result in such chaos that the kids no longer want to play there. They then end up bringing their toys into other rooms. The end result is a cluttered home full of play items and toys.

Getting Started

Start off by determining the kids clutter threshold. This is the amount of clutter (play items) they are allowed to have. Playing is kids' alpha and omega and they easily get attached to toys. To help them determine what to keep and what to let go can be quite exhausting. Coming to a consensus will be tough, but your children will be happier with fewer toys.

Start off with trash

Before reducing the clutter in the rooms, start by getting rid of the trash in the room. Grab a trash bag and let the kids collect any caddie rappers, papers and any other obvious litter. This will get them into the right mindset for the decluttering process.

Simple stuff first

Guide the children to do the easy stuff first. For instance, tell them to 'pick up all the clothes from the floor and to put them in the laundry basket' or 'help me to make the bed'.

Assuming that you have already emptied the shelves, guide them in putting their favorite books on the shelf. Dana White, the author of 'Decluttering at the Speed of Life' calls it the **container concept**. We will also use of this terminology several times in the coming chapters. You can have the shelf divided into sections: one section for the favorites and the other section for the fairly favorites. You can use containers for the relevant categories. Choosing their favorite books will feel like fun and less of a decluttering process. Let them know they have to choose cautiously since the favorite section can only take a limited amount of books. It will result in a less complex struggle to get the remaining items into the other container. If by chance they find another favorite amongst the remaining items, it will not pose a problem: just apply the rule One-In-One-Out. They can put the book in their favorite box only if they remove one a book from the favorite box.

Make use of decluttering questions

Clothes are off the floor and books are on the shelves. Make use of the decluttering questions discussed earlier on in this book. As much as kids wouldn't want to put anything in the donate box or trash bin, the questions will give them as guidance as to what exactly they need to keep.

This is the one question I consider as the deal breaker for children: 'If you needed this item, where would you look for it?'

Help them put the various items they want to keep in the 'place they would look for them if they needed them'. They can put it in the tub, basket, box, etc. If they are unable to answer the question, it means that particular shoe, dress or toy is not important. Let them put it in the donate box or trash bin.

Once all is done, check in the baskets and boxes for the items they were not prepared to lose. If any of these places are already overflowing, you'll need to go initiate another decluttering process. Empty everything from the particular boxes and let the children identify only the favorites and put everything else in the donate bin. Just remember the One-In-One-Out rule if the kids find something they can't afford to lose.

Handling the stuffed animals stress

Every home with kids experiences this problem: oodles of stuffed animals that are never enough. They are beautiful and they provide our kids with the perfect company. But when they are strewn across the room, it becomes a problem.

Help your kids put up a hammock or a shelf that can function as an animal zoo: an animal zoo that should however not be allowed to be crowded. Only a fair number of stuffed animal can be part of the animal zoo. If you find duplicate stuffed animals or animals that the kids' don't care to get rid of, put them in the donate box. And as always, remember the One-In-One-Out rule.

Helping older family members

You might be one of those people who don't like getting into your relatives' lives. Well, I get you. I also dislike getting into the personal space of my relatives: especially when it has to do with a decluttering issue. But again, sometimes it is unavoidable.

Just take into account your grandparents who are in their eighties now and very soon you might have to move to an elderly care facility. Assuming that they have never been keen to practice the decluttering exercise in their own home, you'll obviously be in for a tough job.

You'll be dealing with more than fifty years of accumulated clutter. Uh, tough! But you have one advantage. You have no emotional attachment whatsoever to the stuff in their home.

If it is your parent in laws, it's unlikely that you'll become nostalgic about getting rid of their stuff, since you don't belong there. It will be easy to get rid of things.

However, as you go about everything, remember that your relationship with them still matters. Don't let decluttering get in the way of your relationship with them. It would be wise to avoid giving instructions as to what needs to be trashed and can easily damage your relationship.

Be cautious not to be too personal. This is not the time to remember how much you were hurt back in the days by them. It's not the right time to tell your parents how hurt you felt when you spot that nice jacket your brother received on his eighteenth birthday. Your focus must only be on decluttering now! Your main task is to help them get rid of clutter.

Start by getting rid of the obvious trash that you can discard without any questions. Next, involve them in identifying items that could be stored in the wrong place. Be the muscle and guide them to where they should go.

Since they probably already know which stuff they no longer need, enquire if there's some things they would like to donate. Help them to sort out the items and put the things that are up for donation in the donate box. If you come across items that look like trash, ask their opinion before you throw the stuff out.

As you go about this, be sure to ask them the decluttering questions, as this will make the decluttering exercise easier.

To have several baskets available for this decluttering project, will make your progress faster. Just remember to put similar items together.

Allow your parents to identify their favorites and use the container concept to prioritize items in the elimination process. As much as you want to respect their decisions, make them understand how important space is.

The Challenges You Might Encounter
Hoarding

If you come to realize that your prospects are real keepers, you might need to involve a professional declutterer. Hoarding is not good for their health and safety, so you'll need call for specialized help for them.

Offer to help with the basic work

Your relatives might not be ready to declutter, but there's still some little things you can do. For instance, if they already have a bag of donations they have been preparing to take to the local charity, offer to take it to the charity for them. Or if they have a box full of paper that needs to be shredded, offer to help them take it to an office for shredding.

If they'd rather get a few dollars for their items instead of donating it, help them list the stuff on craigslist, eBay or Amazon. If the house is visibly in a mess, do the dishes, the laundry and clean the house for them.

By doing the basic housework, they'll soon gather courage and give in to your decluttering offer.

Helping Your Spouse

Your friends might not be happy with your decluttering proposal and might therefore cut ties with you. Fine, you can always get new friends.

Kids are kids. They are your juniors. You are in charge and in a position to direct the entire decluttering process. They often have no choice but to follow your guidance.

With senior citizens, respect them and just let them be. If they don't want help, simply accept it. You can't sacrifice a relationship for decluttering.

BUT WITH A SPOUSE IT IS QUITE DIFFERENT.

You are partners. You live in the same house under the same roof. The clutter of your spouse is bothersome to you. The challenge here is that you cannot just get rid of your spouse's clutter without their involvement and consent.

See, with your kids you can announce a specific time for the clearing out of their room and even go ahead and ban all playing activities until the tidying is done. But you can't possibly treat your partner as a child. No adult would tolerate to be treated in that manner.

So where do you start?

Just start decluttering

Go ahead and start decluttering. Clear out your own stuff. Go on and declutter neutral items like towels, cups, etc. Be cautious to only declutter the neutral stuff that belongs to you. Don't dare touch the stuff of your spouse!

Don't start a power struggle

Your partner might not care that the house is in a mess. It's even worse he keeps cluttering your home. But starting a power struggle won't do your relationship any good. Just do your best to control what you can without appearing like you are forcing things. Introduce your partner to the decluttering concept, but don't expect to see results instantly.

Appreciate the progress

You are the decluttering maniac here and he is not. As much as you would like to see results within a short time, appreciate the progress he is making. If he is now able to put dirty clothes in the laundry basket, that's a huge plus. Applaud him for that and help him realize how good it is to live with minimal clutter. You'll be amazed at the change you'll see in his point of view and the grip he is starting to get on things that you thought he would never let go of.

When everything fails, counseling might help

Sometimes problems in a marriage can run deeper than clutter. If both of you cannot communicate your feelings, there is no way you're going to declutter that home. It would be wise to consider seeing a marriage counselor or to read a book about communication in marriage.

CHAPTER 4. HOW TO TURN YOUR CLUTTER INTO CASH

Throughout the previous chapters, we have dived into every aspect of how to deal with your clutter. Most declutter processes ended in donating, giving away to our friends or turning the clutter into cash.

In one of the chapters we determined that people hold onto stuff because of the high amounts of money they spent on that stuff. But who said you can't kill two birds with one stone? It is possible to live in a clutter-free home and still manage to recoup your financial losses.

Everyone loves money (or so I guess). In this chapter we will hence look into ways you can make money and minimize clutter at the same time. Or how else would you be able to compliment yourself after the completion of a tough project like decluttering?

Before the reselling project

The phrase 'I'm going to sell that' has definitely become a very familiar one. You set items aside when decluttering with the intention to sell them someday. And as we have already stated a hundred times, someday never seems to come.

It's time for action. Avoid putting items aside and saying 'I will sell that'. Have specific plans in place! Know where, when and how you will sell your clutter. Remember, you should only sell stuff that have some actual and real value. If you have been hanging onto a faulty blender with intentions of reselling it, too bad - you might never get a buyer.

It's also important that you bear in mind that reselling takes time and if you have a pile of stuff, tit might even take longer. You can consider selling a single item at a time. This will give you ample time to take pictures, upload them on advertisement websites, write product descriptions and to assign the pricing.

Getting Started

Take a close look at what you want to sell? Are the clothes and shoes torn, discolored, stained or do they have small signs of wear and tear? Do the DVDs and CDs have scratches? Is everything else showing signs of excessive usage?

If you answered yes to the above questions, then you are better off donating them to charity organizations or to discard of them.

1. Visit the consignment shops

These shops are quite strict on what they accept. If your items look like they don't stand a good chance of being resold, they simply won't be accepted by them. The items you take to them should not only be clean and in perfect condition, but also trendy and stylish.

And how do these shops work?

They function in two ways. They can buy stuff from you directly and sell them as part of their stock. The second option is for them to take over the items from you and once the stuff sells out, you receive a percentage of the sale price - in most cases 40 to 60 percent.

If you are not sure where to find the consignment shops near you, a local Google search can be of great help.

2. Garage and car boot sales

Garage and car boot sales are a great way to get rid of those random items you have been intending to sell. However, be informed that your effort and time might not really be worth the per hour returns. Maybe that is why most people prefer to resell their stuff on advertisement websites.

However, you can still be successful if you pull it together with other like-minded souls. You can organize a church wide, a town wide or neighborhood wide sale. Advertise the yard sale, as this will help to get the word out there. If you are lucky, a massive influx might just turn up on the day of the sale - all ready and eager to buy your stuff.

3. Craigslist

Craigslist is probably the most straightforward way to sell your possessions. With Craigslist, it's the buyer's responsibility to pick items from the seller. This makes it a perfect place to sell bulky items that could be problematic to move around or to transport, eg, furniture.

However, be extra careful. The fact that a stranger will be showing up at your home, is enough reason to take caution. Just make sure that you will not be all alone in the house at the time of pick up. You'd rather be cautious than sorry!

One last thing about Craigslist - to sell items on Craigslist you will need to sign up, upload clear pictures of your items for sale, list the items and assign reasonable prices to every listed item.

4. Gumtree

This site works similarly to Craigslist. If you live in the United Kingdom, Gumtree is probably a better option for you than Craigslist.

5. eBay

The difference between Craigslist and eBay is the safety aspect. With eBay you do not have to deal with total strangers coming over to your house for the collection of their items. The other difference is that the eBay selling process involves a myriad of steps to follow and complete before your items get listed on their site. Therefore, the site is only ideal if you are selling lots of highly in demand items like dolls, collectible toys, antiques and comic books.

It's also worth noting that you as the seller will be responsible for the shipping of the item to the buyer. Again, this makes it cost effective if you're selling smaller sized items. Large and bulky possessions will just eat up your profit margins, unless you charge the buyer with high shipping charges.

6. Amazon

Just like eBay, Amazon is a great site to sell your collectibles and in demand items. For only $39.99 per month, you can sell and ship items as a professional seller. The second option would be for you to join the Fulfillment by Amazon (FBA). With FBA, you ship the items to Amazon, they store the items and once an item gets sold, Amazon ships it to the customer. Well, Amazon gets to enjoy a bigger chunk from the sale, but you also succeed in getting rid of unwanted stuff in your home - so it's a win-win situation.

CHAPTER 5. FINAL THOUGHTS

By now you should have a strong grasp of what decluttering involves. If you have not started decluttering, it's my belief that you will get into it very soon. However, I can't help but reinforce a few important points.

1. Make it a habit to declutter

The secret of developing a habit isn't how long you work on something, but how consistent you are in applying the habit. No matter how busy you are, fit the declutter habit into your tight schedule. If you can habitually eliminate clutter every time you come across clutter, then you will be assured of living a clutter-free life.

2. Tackle favorite rooms first

Always start off decluttering the rooms where you spend most of your time. It could be the bedroom, office or living room. When decluttered, these rooms will make you relaxed and more motivated to see positive results in the other rooms.

3. This is not a race

Decluttering does not need the fast and furious version of yourself. Be slow, but sure of steady and more sustainable progress. That explains why this book did not once emphasize any set time frame for a decluttering project. Every home is different. Just because you read an article about someone who decluttered their home in 7 days, it doesn't mean decluttering will take you the same amount of time. Don't compare. Don't compete. Make it an adventure and not a race.

4. Small progress is also progress

Celebrate the small milestones. If you are decluttering for the first time, the odds are that you'll not see a huge progress very fast. Learn to celebrate baby steps and the small wins. Be consistent and the big results will soon be evident.

5. Holding on is tougher than letting go

Letting go might make you feel sad, but hanging onto stuff will never give you inner peace. By hanging onto something, you pay for it with money (rent), time, attention and also your emotions. But once you let go, you feel guilty for a day or two and thereafter you get to enjoy peace of mind.

THANK YOU NOTE

Before I let you go, I would like to thank you for reading this book to the very end. Your time is precious and I appreciate that you chose to spend a few hours reading this book.

You could have picked hundreds of other books about decluttering, but you checked out this one. Thank you!

Now that we've reached the end of this amazing book, it's my belief that you are enriched with every bit of information regarding decluttering and every tip as how to start the process.

However, you must be ready to take action - otherwise all the information in this book is worthless. Remember, it's not hard to declutter, all you need is dedication.

Made in the USA
Las Vegas, NV
07 August 2022

52820101R00039